12 REPTILES
BACK FROM THE BRINK

by Samantha S. Bell

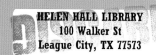

www.12StoryLibrary.com

12-Story Library is an imprint of Peterson Publishing Company and Press Room Editions.

Produced for 12-Story Library by Red Line Editorial

Photographs ©: Frontpage/Shutterstock Images, cover, 1, 16; NHPA/SuperStock, 5; Sergey Lavrentev/Shutterstock Images, 6; Shutterstock Images, 7, 12, 13; John Austin/Shutterstock Images, 9; Ryan M. Bolton/Shutterstock Images, 10, 14, 29; Michiel de Wit/Shutterstock Images, 11, 28; Jacqui Martin/Shutterstock Images, 15; Gerard A. DeBoer/Shutterstock Images, 17; photoiconix/Shutterstock Images, 18; Elena Kalistratova/Shutterstock Images, 19; age fotostock/SuperStock, 21; Czesznak Zsolt/Shutterstock Images, 22; Marek Swadzba/Shutterstock Images, 23; Evgeniapp/Shutterstock Images, 24; You Touch Pix of EuToch/Shutterstock Images, 25; Steve Byland/Shutterstock Images, 26; Leonardo Gonzalez/Shutterstock Images, 27

ISBN
978-1-63235-005-3 (hardcover)
978-1-63235-065-7 (paperback)
978-1-62143-046-9 (hosted ebook)

Library of Congress Control Number: 2014937256

Printed in the United States of America
Mankato, MN
June, 2014

Go beyond the book. Get free, up-to-date content on this topic at 12StoryLibrary.com.

TABLE OF CONTENTS

Giant Lizard of La Gomera 4

Chinese Alligator 6

Western Swamp Tortoise 8

Lake Erie Water Snake 10

Tuatara 12

Ploughshare Tortoise 14

Grand Cayman Blue Iguana 16

Galapagos Giant Tortoise 18

Antiguan Racer Snake 20

Sand Lizard 22

Kemp's Ridley Sea Turtle 24

American Crocodile 26

Fact Sheet 28

Glossary 30

For More Information 31

Index 32

About the Author 32

GIANT LIZARD OF LA GOMERA REDISCOVERED

For more than 500 years, the giant lizards of La Gomera were part of history. Scientists only knew about them from studying fossils. The lizards made history again in 1999. Six of them were discovered on the island of La Gomera, off the coast of Morocco.

The large lizards move slowly. Scientists believe cats and rats killed many of them. People might

IUCN RED LIST

The International Union for the Conservation of Nature (IUCN) keeps a list of all threatened species in the world, called the Red List. Each species is labeled according to how at risk it is.

Least Concern: Not considered at risk.

Near Threatened: At risk of being vulnerable or endangered in the future.

Vulnerable: At risk of extinction.

Endangered: At high risk of extinction.

Critically Endangered: At extremely high risk of extinction.

Extinct in the Wild: Only lives in captivity.

Extinct: No members of a species are left.

The giant lizards of La Gomera grow to be up to four feet (1.2 m) long.

have hunted them, too. The lizards probably had a large habitat long ago. But the six remaining lizards were found on just two rocky cliffs.

Scientists caught the lizards. Then they started a breeding program. More and more lizards were born each year. In 2011, more than 260 lizards lived in captivity. Scientists also removed the predators from the habitat. They made plans to release some lizards back onto the island.

500
Number of years scientists thought these lizards were extinct.

Status: Critically endangered
Population: More than 90 in the wild
Home: La Gomera Island
Life Span: Unknown

CHINESE ALLIGATORS THRIVING IN NEW HOME

Chinese alligators are thought to have inspired the dragons in Chinese legends. But these alligators aren't fierce. Chinese alligators hunt for clams, snails, and fish. Sometimes they catch small birds or mammals. They aren't dangerous to people. But people's actions have threatened them.

The alligators lived in the wetlands around the Yangtze River in China. The fertile land there was also perfect for growing rice. As the number of rice farmers increased, the habitat for the alligators grew smaller. By the early 1900s, Chinese alligators could only be found at the lower end of the river. By the

Chinese alligators usually hunt at night and rest during the day.

The Chinese alligator is much smaller than its cousin, the American alligator.

end of the century, the alligators had lost more than 90 percent of their habitat.

To save the alligators, scientists started a breeding program. The Chinese Alligator Breeding Research Center started with approximately 200 alligators. In 2009, it had more than 10,000. The alligators are also raised in zoos and wildlife refuges. The first three alligators were released into the wild in 2003. In 2007, six more were released.

5

Length in feet (1.5 m) of a typical Chinese alligator.

Status: Critically endangered
Population: 150 in the wild
Home: Yangtze River, China
Life Span: Approximately 50 years

TIME TO HIBERNATE

During the winter, Chinese alligators in the wild hibernate deep in the mud. But the ponds at the breeding center are made of concrete. Workers must move all the alligators into warm indoor rooms when it's cold.

WESTERN SWAMP TORTOISE MAKING SLOW BUT STEADY COMEBACK

Many animals hibernate during the winter. But the western swamp tortoise becomes more active in cold weather. It hibernates through the hot summer. The tortoises lost their habitat when Australia's swampland dried up year-round.

The tortoises live in certain swamps in Australia. These swamps fill up with water for only a short time each year. The tortoises swim and eat in the water. But much of the land has been drained for farming or development. In other places, wildfires destroyed the swampland. Cats, rats, and foxes also killed many of the tortoises. By the early 1980s, only 20 to 30 western swamp tortoises were left in the wild.

The Australian government stepped in to help. It set aside land for wildlife refuges. Scientists bred and raised the tortoises in a zoo. Since 1988, they have released more than 500 tortoises into their new habitats.

THINK ABOUT IT

Why do you think some animals hibernate during summer? Why do others hibernate through winter?

6

Months out of the year that a swamp tortoise is active.

Status: Critically endangered
Population: Approximately 300 in the wild
Home: Australian swamps
Life Span: 60–70 years

Western swamp tortoises eat tadpoles and frogs, which used to be plentiful during the wet season.

LAKE ERIE WATER SNAKE SLITHERS TO SAFETY

When summer tourists visit the Lake Erie Islands off the shores of northern Ohio, they might not expect to see snakes. But sometimes they see a whole pile of them. The Lake Erie water snakes lay in the sun on the rocky shores. They gather in large groups there for breeding. The snakes weren't always so easy to find, however.

Lake Erie water snakes live on cliffs and rocky ledges during the summer.

SNAKES HELPING PEOPLE

In the 1990s, cargo ships accidentally brought goby fish into Lake Erie. They were in the ballast water that helps those ships stay balanced. The ships released some of the water into the lake. The gobies entered the lake, too. Gobies eat the eggs of the other fish that fishers like to catch. As water snake populations grew, they ate the gobies. Now the snakes have plenty of food, and people can still go fishing.

The snakes will bite if threatened, but they are not poisonous. People who lived on the islands feared them anyway. They killed thousands of snakes. Houses, resorts, and other development also destroyed the snakes' shoreline habitat.

In 1999, the snakes were listed as endangered. It became illegal to kill or harm them. By that time, approximately 2,000 snakes were

23
Average number of snakelets in a litter.

Status: Least concern
Population:
   Approximately 12,000
Home: Lake Erie Islands
Life Span: Unknown

Lake Erie water snakes range in length from 1.5 to 3.5 feet (0.5–1.1 m) long.

left. Conservationists tagged and studied them. They educated residents so they would not fear the snakes. By 2011, approximately 12,000 Lake Erie water snakes were slithering on the islands again.

TUATARA SET TO RETURN TO NEW ZEALAND

Tuataras have been around for 225 million years. They were alive when dinosaurs roamed the earth. Tuataras live in burrows during the day and hunt at night. They eat frogs, insects, and worms. They often share their burrows with sea birds. Tuataras used to be found all around the mainland and islands of New Zealand.

Settlers from nearby islands first arrived in New Zealand approximately 700 years ago. Rats arrived with the settlers. The rats ate the tuataras. By the 1840s, tuataras were almost extinct on the mainland. As ships traveled to the islands, the rats spread. Tuataras became extinct on some of these

Tuataras look like lizards, but they have no ears, and they live in cooler climates than lizards.

Tuataras' closest relative is an extinct group of reptiles that lived at the same time as the dinosaurs did.

islands as well. Most recently, they disappeared from Whenuakura Island in approximately 1984.

In the mid-1980s, scientists used poison pellets to rid the islands of rats. They collected tuatara eggs and hatched them in captivity. They also caught adults to start breeding programs. By 2012, almost all of the tuataras' islands were free of rats. Scientists have started releasing tuataras back into the wild.

THINK ABOUT IT

When an animal or plant is brought to a place where it didn't live before, it is called an invasive species. What are some ways an invasive species could affect a habitat? What do you think should be done about invasive species?

4

Number of years that pass before a female tuatara lays another group of eggs.

Status: Least concern
Population: 50,000–100,000
Home: New Zealand and surrounding islands
Life Span: More than 80 years

13

PLOUGHSHARE TORTOISES RETURN TO MADAGASCAR

The ploughshare tortoise has an unusual shell. The lower shell sticks out between the tortoise's front legs. Males use their shells to try to knock each other over. The winner mates with the female.

Ploughshare tortoises used to be common on Madagascar, an island country off the coast of Africa. Then humans destroyed much of the tortoises' habitat. Farmers cleared the land by burning it.

Some tortoises died in the fires. People brought bush pigs from the mainland. Bush pigs started to prey on the tortoise eggs and hatchlings. Poachers also caught the tortoises illegally. They sold them to collectors in Asia.

In 1986, scientists started a breeding center with eight tortoises. The government set aside 22 square miles (57 sq km) as a national park. Local residents trapped the bush

Ploughshare tortoises eat mainly grasses and small shrubs.

Ploughshare tortoises are native to Baly Bay, an area of northwestern Madagascar that has swamps, forests, and savannas.

pigs. Law officers cracked down on tortoise poaching. In the meantime, the breeding program had some success. In 2009, the breeding center housed 17 adults and 200 juveniles. Scientists released the first 20 tortoises back into the wild in 2011.

237
Average number of days tortoise eggs take to hatch.

Status: Critically endangered
Population: Fewer than 400 in the wild
Home: Madagascar
Life Span: 50–100 years

A PERMANENT MARK

Poachers still try to sell the tortoises to collectors. Juveniles sell for approximately $1,000. Adults sell for almost $30,000. To stop the sales, conservationists are marking the tortoises. Numbers and letters are engraved into their shells. Conservationists hope collectors will not want to buy the tortoises that have markings. The marks also make it easier for officials to find the tortoises if they are poached.

LAND SET ASIDE FOR GRAND CAYMAN BLUE IGUANA

The Grand Cayman blue iguana has gray-blue skin. It turns bright blue when other iguanas are near. It makes itself brighter to lay a claim to its territory. The blue iguanas are the largest lizards on Grand Cayman Island, a small island in the Caribbean Sea. They can grow up to five feet (1.5 m) in length and can weigh as much as 25 pounds (11.3 kg). These large reptiles had few predators until people arrived.

When people moved to the island, they brought their cats and dogs. The iguanas didn't have a natural fear of the animals. They didn't run away. The cats and dogs killed the iguanas. Others were hit by cars. By 2002, only 10 to 25 iguanas were left.

The Grand Cayman blue iguana lives by itself except when breeding.

GRAND CAYMAN GREEN IGUANAS

Green iguanas also live on the island. People brought them as pets from Central and South America. Green iguanas had natural predators before moving to the island. Unlike the blue iguanas, the green iguanas knew to run away from the cats and dogs. They also reproduced quickly. Now there are too many green iguanas.

45
Number of different plant species the iguana will eat.

Status: Endangered
Population: 750 in the wild
Home: Grand Cayman Island
Life Span: 25–40 years

In the 1990s, conservationists stepped in to help. They bred and raised iguanas in captivity. Hundreds were released back into wildlife refuges. There they are safe from threats, such as cars and pets. In 2013, approximately 750 blue iguanas were living in the wild.

The blue iguana has a spiky crest that begins at the base of the neck and goes to the end of the tail.

GALAPAGOS GIANT TORTOISE SAVED FROM RATS

Galapagos giant tortoises use very little energy. They can live up to a year without eating or drinking. They nap almost 16 hours a day. They spend their waking hours eating and basking in the sun on Pinzon Island and other Galapagos Islands off the coast of Ecuador. When the tortoises find water, they drink large amounts and store it inside their bodies. An invasion of rats more than 100 years ago threatened their quiet existence.

At that time, pirates and fishers came to Pinzon Island. Black rats arrived on the ships, too. The rats ate the tortoise eggs and hatchlings. By the 1950s, only approximately 200 adult giant tortoises could be found.

Galapagos giant tortoises are one of the largest tortoise species.

Galapagos giant tortoises have a good sense of smell. They smell grasses and plants when deciding which ones to eat.

5

Age a tortoise is large enough to be safe from predators.

Status: Vulnerable
Population: More than 500 on Pinzon Island; 15,000 throughout the Galapagos Islands
Home: Galapagos Islands
Life Span: 100–150 years

In 1965, scientists began gathering eggs. They raised the hatchlings for approximately five years. At that age, scientists released them into the wild. Since the program started, scientists have released more than 550 tortoises. But 180 million rats still lived on Pinzon Island. In 2012, scientists succeeded in poisoning the rats. Now the tortoises can nest safely.

ANTIGUAN RACER SNAKES MAKE A COMEBACK

Antiguan racer snakes are small and harmless. That is, unless you are a lizard. The snakes ambush lizards by hiding under leaves. Only the snakes' heads stick out. But the predators soon became the prey. The snakes were almost wiped out with the arrival of two invasive species to the Caribbean island of Antigua.

In the 1800s, rats came on ships and ate the snakes. Farmers also brought in mongooses to kill the snakes in their fields. By 1995, only 50 Antiguan racer snakes could be found on one small island.

That same year, conservation groups joined together to save the snakes. They set up a breeding program. They also taught the local residents not to fear or kill the snakes. Then they removed the mongooses and rats from Antigua. Snakes were released into their new, safe habitats. By 2010, more than 500 Antiguan racer snakes lived in the wild.

SAVING MORE THAN SNAKES

Removing the rats and mongooses from the islands helped other animals, too. There used to be only two breeding pairs of Caribbean brown pelicans. By 2010, more than 60 lived there. The white-crowned pigeons have increased from just five breeding pairs to more than 450. Sea turtle and lizard eggs are also safe from rats. Even the plants on the islands have recovered.

39
Typical length in inches (1 m) of an adult female.

Status: Critically endangered

Population: More than 500 in the wild

Home: Antigua and Barbuda

Life Span: More than 15 years

Antiguan racer snakes are harmless to humans. Their only defense is to release a smell when frightened.

SAND LIZARDS RETURN TO SAND DUNES

Sand lizards are Great Britain's only egg-laying lizards. They lay their eggs in the bare sand. The sun warms the eggs until they hatch late in the summer. When the sand dunes began to disappear, the lizards did, too.

Development destroyed much of the lizards' habitat. In other areas, scrub pines and non-native plants created too much shade. The eggs wouldn't hatch without the sun's warmth. By the 1960s, the lizards had become extinct in the wild.

Sand lizards eat insects, spiders, worms, and slugs.

The green specks on male sand lizards become brighter in breeding season.

In 1995, zoo workers, conservationists, and volunteers began breeding and raising sand lizards. They worked to restore habitat sites. They cleared away plants and created sandy patches for the eggs. By 2013, more than 9,000 lizards had been released back into the wild.

9

Average number of eggs a female lizard lays at one time.

Status: Least concern
Population: More than 9,000 raised in captivity and released in Great Britain
Home: Great Britain and other European and Asian countries
Life Span: Approximately 12 years

THINK ABOUT IT

Sand lizards are found in other countries in Europe. Why was it important to bring the lizards back to Great Britain? Would you have worked so hard to bring them back to one particular area?

NESTING SITES OF KEMP'S RIDLEY SEA TURTLES PROTECTED

Hundreds or thousands of Kemp's Ridley sea turtles gather all at once for nesting. Scientists think they nest in groups as a defense against predators. In the 1940s, tens of thousands gathered on one beach on the Gulf of Mexico to nest. By the 1980s, only approximately 300 females were found on the same beach laying their eggs. The turtles were heading for extinction.

Over the years, people took the turtle eggs to eat and sell. Fishers accidentally caught grown turtles in their shrimp nets. The turtles got tangled in the nets and drowned. Their numbers steadily went down.

Kemp's Ridley sea turtles are one of the smallest sea turtle species.

Kemp's Ridley sea turtles swim in shallow waters, feeding on crabs and other shellfish.

Mexico and the United States worked together to help. In the 1970s, both countries passed laws to protect nesting sites. From 1978 to 1988, scientists gathered eggs and raised the turtles.

When they were 9 to 11 months old, the turtles were released. In 2009, more than 21,000 nests were found in the wild.

3

Number of times the turtle might nest in a season.

Status: Critically endangered
Population: Approximately 1,000 breeding females
Home: Gulf of Mexico
Life Span: Approximately 50 years

ESCAPE PLAN

In the 1990s, new laws required special devices on shrimp fishing nets. The devices help the turtles to escape if they are caught in the nets. These devices are made of metal bars. The shrimp pass through the bars into a bag. The turtles are too big to go through. The bars are slanted, and the turtle moves along them to an opening in the net.

HABITAT RESTORED FOR AMERICAN CROCODILE

The American crocodile stays completely still when it hunts. As its prey comes closer, the crocodile grabs it with its powerful jaws. When people moved into their habitats, however, American crocodiles couldn't protect themselves.

The crocodiles lived in bays and marshes in south Florida. In the

1860s, settlers arrived and cleared the land for farming. Over the next century, they drained the swampland

The American crocodile is one of the largest crocodile species in the world.

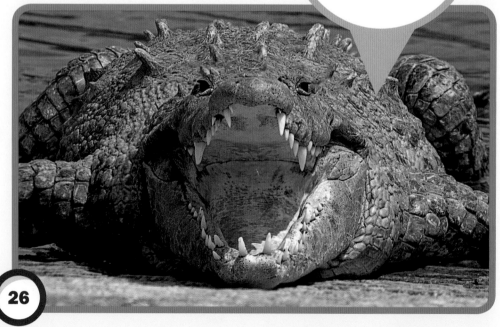

American crocodiles occasionally attack people, but usually they flee if they see humans.

and developed the land where crocodiles nested. Hunters shot the crocodiles and sold their hides. By the 1970s, between 200 and 400 crocodiles were left in the wild.

77

Average number of teeth in a crocodile's mouth.

Status: Vulnerable
Population:
    Approximately 1,500 in Florida
Home: Florida, Central and South America
Life Span: Approximately 45 years

Habitats have been maintained for the crocodiles in Florida's Everglades National Park. In 1980, the government created another wildlife refuge in Key Largo, Florida. The crocodiles also have started nesting in a third spot near a nuclear power plant. The canals around the plant provide plenty of food. The water levels stay constant. There are no people around. By 2012, approximately 1,500 crocodiles were living in Florida.

FACT SHEET

- Reptiles are cold-blooded animals with a backbone, lungs for breathing, and tough skin with scales. Reptiles include lizards, snakes, turtles, crocodilians, and tuataras.

- There are 8,240 species of reptiles in the world. Reptiles can be found on every continent except Antarctica.

- More than 4,000 reptile species had been evaluated by the IUCN Red List of Threatened Species. One reptile species, the black softshell turtle, is extinct in the wild. Another 164 reptiles were critically endangered, and 329 were endangered.

- The main threats to reptiles include habitat loss and climate change. Some species are also threatened by non-native predators, such as rats, and the pet trade.

- Many countries have laws protecting endangered animals. In 1973, the US Congress passed the Endangered Species Act. It requires state and federal government agencies to monitor and protect species that might become extinct. It also bans people from hunting, catching, trading, or possessing animals and plants that are protected.

- Reptiles cannot control their own body heat. They must depend on warmth from the sun.

- Most reptiles lay eggs. Some give birth to live babies called neonates.

- Some turtles and tortoises can live for more than 100 years.

- Only a few hundred of the 3,000 snake species are venomous. In the United States, these include rattlesnakes, copperheads, cottonmouths, and coral snakes.

GLOSSARY

breeding
The process by which animals or plants are produced by their parents.

conservationist
A person who tries to protect natural resources.

development
The building of houses or structures on a piece of land.

dune
A hill of sand piled up by the wind.

endangered
Threatened with extinction.

extinct
The death of all members of a species.

habitat
The place where a plant or animal naturally lives or grows.

hibernate
To spend a season in a resting or sleeping state.

non-native
Plants or animals that do not naturally occur in a certain location.

predator
An animal that kills or eats another animal.

prey
An animal that is killed or eaten by another animal.

species
A group of animals or plants that are similar and can produce young.

wetlands
Land or areas such as marshes or swamps that have a lot of soil moisture.

FOR MORE INFORMATION

Books

Boothroyd, Jennifer. *Endangered and Extinct Reptiles*. Minneapolis, MN: Lerner, 2014.

Everything You Need to Know about Snakes and Other Scaly Reptiles. New York: DK Children, 2013.

Haywood, Karen. *Crocodiles and Alligators*. New York: Benchmark Books, 2010.

Llewellyn, Claire. *Reptiles*. London: Kingfisher, 2013.

McCarthy, Colin. *Reptile*. New York: DK Children, 2010.

Websites

Discovery Kids: Reptiles
kids.discovery.com/tell-me/animals/reptiles

Kiwi Conservation Club: Reptiles and Amphibians
www.kcc.org.nz/reptiles-and-amphibians

National Geographic: Reptiles
animals.nationalgeographic.com/animals/reptiles

San Diego Zoo Kids: Reptiles.
adminkids.sandiegozoo.org/animals/reptiles

INDEX

American crocodiles, 26–27

Antiguan racer snakes, 20–21

Australia, 8

breeding programs, 5, 7, 8, 13, 14–15, 17, 19, 20, 23, 25

Caribbean Sea, 16, 20

China, 6–7

Chinese alligators, 6–7

Ecuador, 18

Everglades National Park, 27

farmland, 6, 8, 14, 20, 26

Florida, 26, 27

fossils, 4

Galapagos giant tortoises, 18–19

giant lizards of La Gomera, 4–5

Grand Cayman blue iguanas, 16–17

Grand Cayman green iguanas, 17

Great Britain, 22, 23

Gulf of Mexico, 24

hibernation, 7, 8

hunting, 5, 27

Kemp's Ridley sea turtles, 24–25

Lake Erie water snakes, 10–11

Madagascar, 14

Mexico, 25

Morocco, 4

New Zealand, 12

ploughshare tortoises, 14–15

poaching, 14–15

rats, 4, 8, 12–13, 18–19, 20

sand lizards, 22–23

tuataras, 12–13

western swamp tortoises, 8–9

wildfires, 8

wildlife refuges, 7, 8, 17, 27

Yangtze River, 6

About the Author

Samantha Bell is a graduate of Furman University and has taught writing and art to both children and adults. She has written or illustrated more than 20 books for children.

READ MORE FROM 12-STORY LIBRARY

Every 12-Story Library book is available in many formats, including Amazon Kindle and Apple iBooks. For more information, visit your device's store or 12StoryLibrary.com.